JOURNEYS

Special edition

Karl Hicken

ISBN 978-1-967362-13-4 (paperback)
ISBN 978-1-967362-14-1 (hardcover)
ISBN 978-1-967362-15-8 (digital)

Printed in the United States of America

DEDICATION

This book is dedicated to those who recognize life's infirmities and develop a desire to give a better life to the ones who love them. Further, a sincere dedication, to my wife, and to my family, for never giving up on me.

Contents

Journey 1..1
Journey 2..1
Journey 3..2
Journey 4..2
Journey 5..3
Journey 6..4
Journey 7..4
Journey 8..5
Journey 9..5
Journey 10..6
Journey 11..7
Journey 12..7
Journey 13..8
Journey 14..8
Journey 15..10
Journey 16..10
Journey 17..11
Journey 18..12
Journey 19..12
Journey 20..13
Journey 21..14
Journey 22..14
Journey 23..15
Journey 24..16
Journey 25..16
Journey 26..17
Journey 27..17
Journey 28..18

Journey 29...19
Journey 30...20
Journey 31...20
Journey 32...21
Journey 33...22
Journey 34...23
Journey 35...23
Journey 36...24
Journey 37...25
Journey 38...27
Journey 39...28
Journey 40...28
Journey 41...29
Journey 42...29
Journey 43...30
Journey 44...31
Journey 45...32
Journey 46...32
Journey 47...33
Journey 48...34
Journey 49...34
Journey 50...35
Journey 51...36
Journey 52...37
Journey 53...38
Journey 54...39
Journey 55...39
Journey 56...40
Journey 57...41
Journey 58...42
Journey 59...43
Journey 60...44
Journey 61...44
Journey 62...45
Journey 63...46
Journey 64...46

Journey 65..47
Journey 66..48
Journey 67..48
Journey 68..50
Journey 69..51
Journey 70..51
Journey 71..52
Journey 72..53
Journey 73..55
Journey 74..55
Journey 75..56
Journey 76..56
Journey 77..57
Journey 78..58
Journey 79..59
Journey 80..59
Journey 81..61
Journey 82..62
Journey 83..63
Journey 84..63
Journey 85..64
Journey 86..65
Journey 87..66
Journey 88..67
Journey 89..68
Journey 90..69
Journey 91..70
Journey 92..70
Journey 93..71
Journey 94..72
Journey 95..72
Journey 96..73
Journey 97..74

JOURNEY 1

Eyes closed to sight chasing truth from behind the hidden, the forbidden, the unforgiven. Pain and hate crowd hopes and dreams, emptiness prevails. Unwanted destinations buried under a Swirling vortex of dirty clouds that shroud and protect secret places-places of the child, innocent, piercing, seeing without sight left there, not knowing, ever gazing into the stillness eyes, once bright, fair and blue now matted and framed, forgotten no light reaching dimmed from within, shunned from without trapping and holding shards of fears ever present alone.

JOURNEY 2

Shadows of carefully forgotten wishes wrestle for the right to be, just a glimpse of that dreamy land, and the fragrance of imagination. Worthy ideals of the child stir the sullen intensity to grapple with the sentinels that guard the secrets of forever-forever, hmmm, self created and protected forged by strands of lies to be strong not knowing, so willing to be concealed. Guardians, unchallenged, unflinching... not real Imaginary rulers of dark treasures sabers of thought allowed to be believable, powerful, yet none with substance... Aah, but as the suns first rays crest the virgin morn, Sure, truth's hope beckons the attention of the heart, still searching, still sorting.

JOURNEY 3

3 Traveling through vicissitudes of what appears as time lines of consciousness once rigid melt into the haze of thought Drifting and wanting, tollgates passing, Dark, cold staircase, dusty vents that stinging words escape through residues of guilt find residence there. Tender heart, young and vulnerable. Wincing to words ill conceived, yet spoken, with a plainness, a clarity undeniable. Somber authors unaware, slumber warily at night, darkness quells the drama of evening. Expressions that found a mark, find solace in the quiet. Devoid of malice, still unresolved, meld to the tapestry, shaping the life. Now tucked away, stored with the others, There is peace in knowing, as shadows close in, youth and hope will rise united tomorrow.

JOURNEY 4

A more peaceful adult world becomes child's play viewed from the innocence of five. The cold asphalt streets of the city warm to the pleasures of friends. 'T'was the rich adventures of the ice cream man, no costs, no harm, everyone buys happily from Janice and me. Converging on the familiar institution of marriage scorning and mocking the pretense of the players, knowing still that we, the youthful players are also the Pretenders. Frivolous and proud of our moments, the warm afternoons pale to the glow of early love. Teasing and retreating, chasing a million smiles still bashful and giddy, eyes meeting to say, "All of forever is you." But the shadows of the mountain vistas creep into our day and the familiar voices, inaudible, beckon us home. Those forever's make us rich at five, lucid as to its certainty, larger than life memories loom, most pleasing.

JOURNEY 5

Someone must one day explain to me how strange relationships that transcend mortality allow the evil and fear of the unholy dark One to become manifest without invitation, nor even knowledge. No welcome overture, no grand entrance, "Excuse me, I don't even know you." Not sure I even know of you, much less can I abide you now. How dare you come, permeating into what is my little boy. So full of you, he is, that he runs for shelter, Diminutive, paralyzed, in a dream, fighting, falling, finding no respite, How does he run now from what is him? Maybe find a place, guarded and alone, fortified, without access. The hidden, the terrified, consumed with such early anger, hate, piercing family ties, creating unholy fire and immersing self O God, how could you?

Eternal Father, God of Love Great Medium, Intercessor, Agent of all, do you see me? Do you see what I was then? You sent me, promised me, delivered me. And I came, trusting, cradled by angels, yet so ill prepared, and so vulnerable. Veils of glory yield to the haze of unknowing, forgetting, light ebbs into darkness, confusion, enter Satan, I invite. "Hide here," beckons the voice, enticing a cloak of doubt. Ancillary truths, no, not true, take precedence. Easier than the truth, I think. Who did you say you were? My brother, must be ok, yes, come, stay. Cache of unhallowed hope, sequestered by hints of verity, and I succumb to me. Father, Mother, temporal instruments of protection and love, Strained faith of a child, reach for you and the ante mortal promise of peace. Can you hear me? I have not the words, nor the means to make you listen. My utterance moves in waves of silence, penetrating chords of quiet stillness. It is not your fault. Did you ever know me? Will you know me now or ever? Why is this love?

JOURNEY 6

Send me to school, clothe me in your world. Quiet, please, take your seat, don't forget your lunch. Fred and Barney dress up and envelope cold bologna and a slightly bruised banana. No one really eats those, do they? What trade will an injured banana bring? Cold milk in a glass thermos, mmmm, broken cookies, broken thermos. Four cents for school milk, kinda warm but worth it. The smell of the schoolyard, distinct, yet what is it? Not sweet, not pungent, just there. Watching the tricky bars, no friends there, only kindergarten girls hanging from their knees. Colorful shorts, bruises and scrapes, keep looking. Steeliest and cat's eyes, kings of asphalt marbles. Safe entry, a few to lose, chance the win. Lunch recess draws to finale. Ditch the banana, stuff the baggies into my pocket, good for another lunch, maybe tomorrow.

JOURNEY 7

Gray, yet curiously bright, the horizon viewed from my perch on Grandpa's knee. Scratchy collars on my cheek, wire frame glasses clutched between weathered fingers. His voice is firm and soft, his words fill me with the urge to understand. Setting the glasses back to his nose, he points, the white picket fence, the two large bushes crowding the red sidewalk on either side. Then a cloud, peaceful, fluffy, trailing wisps over the big mountain, far away. Farther still, Grandpa, where did you go? Without the wits to know, I miss that touch. There are others, although not the same, our moment in mortality has stayed with me, unmatched, untainted, easy, and true. Some days the clouds bring you back, bring me back to that ethereal touch. Knowing you, feeling that firm, soft voice, come to me pure and peaceful. Love transcendent, spoken words unknown, forgotten, after all, I'm just barely yearling.

JOURNEY 8

Swirling clotheslines, backyard sand pile, croquet set all wrong. Summer vacation is seemingly endless. Siblings finding mindless play most satisfying, then fade. Lying on my back in the soft green of grass, passive scents drift by, earthy, musty. Clotheslines sway and cross under the big wires to create puzzle pieces, undefined, never meant to fit together, tranquil, elusive, evasive geometric shapes chasing visiting clouds, fleeting and nebulous, not to be caught. Armies of ants brave the staggering heights of the uncut grass, why? Some carry remnants of lunch, some tote another, while some bear both. Turning onto my side, upsetting the precarious chain, sending them scurrying for cover. Focus returns to the project at hand, perpetual, futile, blindly efficacious. Lost now in a low ebb of thought, streaming teasing reality, restored consciousness reveals the bulbous shape of a warrior, willing to die, to give all for society. Serenity becomes stinging pain, this hero ant striking fast, searing tears come to my eyes, the martyr shrinks to my blow, we both lose.

JOURNEY 9

A thrift store watch hanging on my second grade wrist, the band worn and stretched with unmeasured age. Time stays the same, 9:38, neither morn or dark of night knows this worthless timepiece.

Immovable, rusted shaft refuses to threaten this ageless reckoning of time. Used and ugly, scratched and stained now, deemed useless. It is my first watch, I don't care. Watching and drifting to slow moving schoolroom clocks, anxious, the time approaches and I believe all need the moment to see, to witness. Everyday I wait 'til 9:38 to show someone this treasure, my watch. Interest heightened, I marvel at this material world. Even time carries no value, not really, like the watch.

The world so carefully measures and grades us, while speculating before and aft, assuming such noble assertions. 9:38, stuck, arrested, paralyzed, and yet nothing changes. Revealing the relative merit of a time charged people. Musing on the thought, I shall find a way to challenge this notion of assigning each a definitive time bound role. This junk store watch adorning my arm and me. The day comes for the old watch to renew and judge, and those who chose decrees to be rendered ever so trivial.

JOURNEY 10

Torpid memories, cunning visage, enchantment of time, releasing and creating reality. Capers and sensation find bold new expression in words. Storytellers, ancient and audacious, finding audience in reciting pleas petitioning the senses of the listener. Sleepy and faded glimpses find life through the artful orator, truth inconsequential, even colorless, yarns spun for what? Varied motives, premeditated, poignant, benefactors of talented tongues, prey on eager followers. Is that bad? Amused at the wisdom, seeming power, logic we ascribe to those pretending to cradle what the masses crave? Pondering, I revel in the thought that maybe I know too, this practiced knowledge, spewed forcefully, lighting on ears that need to hear and grasp or fall. Grappling for believers, motives vacillate, values fade in favor of honor, recognition, and wealth. Pretended allure, painstaking illusions of faith, these tellers of tales capture and captivate. These expressions, do they bless or curse?

JOURNEY 11

Ravaged with the intensity of unbridled fury, rational moments flee as a nervous puppy too well acquainted with its master, never knowing its own miserable fate. Rage courses through vessels ignited with unquenchable fires Welling forth its ill will to punish and hurt. Torrents of anger flow fueled with venomous vitality Know no turning points, only the dense cloak of lies. Blithe and otherwise content figures serve as unwitting servants to this heat of devouring anguish. Fervor and passion bow to gods of melancholy canon. Reason fades with each plane descended Through, Alternatives plead for antidotes, find only levels of Unconquerable quiet. Grave and listless stillness find place as nebulous hues Of gray, satiating, inviting, final.

JOURNEY 12

Tardy bell sounds from distant school provoking first response from capricious young'ens

Poking and toppling each other. So much to prove, so much of nothing to gain. Vanguards of adolescent antics Labor exhaustively for an elusive, hopeful glance. A fleeting chance, maybe an accident with purpose Yes, that's it…an accident feigned to catch the eye of Maybe someone who will notice, Pay some regard. Silly games acted out on schoolyard asphalt, seen from the front row, room 19, east wing. Ms. O'Connor makes her presence known, thundering vocal reclaiming announcement, lighting in the midst of each individual day dream. Radio outside playing 'Happy together', I wonder who writes such melodious strains, then duck to avoid the projectile know as the 'retriever', Feared eraser finds its mark. Musing abruptly comes to consciousness, I return the

JOURNEY 13

Spiraling anguish, limits pressed, no place to retreat when already withdrawn. Halls lined with faceless names, translucent eyes fixed on the end of perspective. The point where infinity meets destiny. Then, for a first blush of eternity, the furthest distance is within reach. Gyrating through self imposed confines, light indelibly fuses with time. Instant horizons appear on impulse, euphoria fill the voids of another day's vain ambition forgotten. Visions of long held belief fade, some real, some barren and hollow. Sacred places where the soul may soar timeless, blessed dwellings of dreams. Gently bestowed, benevolently imparted, earned by one's own most heartless master, the heart.

JOURNEY 14

It becomes time again as life's events give a day of pleasure. Tracing roots from the desert Samaritan from a grand, young Mother, a hopeful, humble birth. Large in body with a towering spirit, trailing peace and perfect love. He came, his eyes of azure sunset, full of savor, teeming with delight. Early years, bumps and scrapes, a football fellow, a helmet of yellow. No limits to the mischief, no appliance or rooftop to imposing to scale. Such a smile, to win the world. Ah, the wonder of his world, so rich, so innocent and true. Eager, we embrace this enchantment. Contagious Joy and bliss, natural and warm, scintillating, sparkling, defining. Oh, but then dark clouds of adolescence crept in, innocence under siege, marauding, a dark pretender comes, daunting, veiling, haunting. This radiant soul shadowed and betrayed, phantoms of dusk stalk the azure hues, dimming, lulling, masking the fervent glow, challenging the eternal hope of this soul.

Returning Tho as the grace of a pristine day dawns, Slivers of early sun perforate the night. Inexorable strength of spirit summons the advent Of a more hallowed dawn. More lustrous from each stripe earned in the darkness. Favored now by the stings of wisdom's lessons gathered, Blessings envelop this sojourn, Nourished with discernment, new found faith, love. Too many moves, so many people, Each with purpose, give and take, endowments to the forging of the man. Silent come the gift bearers, humble, noble, abiding the travail. Patient, determined standard bearers sheathed as Teachers, Leaders, friends, adversaries, enemies. Abstractly void of pretense, presumption. Comes now emergence, an unveiling, a veritable connecting of the dots. Bridges of prudence fill the expanse of youth Giving value to each bump, each scrape. Heightening the bliss, easing the betrayal chasing the shadows, soaring on wings of charity. Formed and founded, all but a pathway. To the now, the beginning. Go now, seek the peace that surpasses understanding, elusive on a fair day, evasive as dark clouds gather. If ever a blessing might be coveted, above them all, seek this, aspire to this. Scaffolds and supports, plentiful and abundant, singly and collectively are but no more than personal decree. Celestial hands bless you in your worthy pursuit, His grace tarries at your feet, glorious destiny beckons.

JOURNEY 15

Rivulets of steam rise through the still night air in a stealthful, planned ascent. Unsuspecting crescent moon rims the sandstone dawn Unequaled in the dark heaven. Towering pines interrupt and pirate the richness, In a swagger, fully believing in their own superiority. Hoary bog, resplendent and enchanting, Waging an eternal contest, seizing strength, breathing life, Proud, confident, giving more than they take in their vie. Grim reaper stalks the radiance of the darkness, poised and shrouded in the lush mosses of the mire. Clinging to the dampness of arms unsunned, Dank fingers know only impending doom. Our walk, makes us shiver, I squeeze the tiny hand Of one who believes and sees as I say. Conjures of spooks and spectral phantasms, wondrously seen, poignantly sensed together. As real as we choose, yet safe and warm as holding hands.

JOURNEY 16

Aversely carrying the weight of life gone awry, I search for what may be genuine in me. What possible flattery may substitute for the best of Bad roads? Filled with the fatigue of self fulfillment, These jaded eyes lose focus.. I run, paralyzed as in a dream, weighted, groggy, as the features of my face slough into the mass. Countless souls, graduated and purposed, stream by, In a cadence of sound, reveling as waves of existence Pour through the medians, Slow and defining as they reach me. I grip the normalcy, the reality of this determined mob, Clinging to the slurry of the path I tread. Outstretched, patronizing lines come from lips, beguiling, But, oh so sure that their well heeled roots command respect. Fear of separation finds lodging deep as the parade Moves on. No prints, no evidence of credible or tangible truth follow, the tragedy of transience, I see, no luminance, no need. Stains of hurt decry the wretch, turn to forgive, fade To shadows. Arise from this soup of premeditated pity, don the Cape of the holy, Reach for, aspire to, pray the dream to end, close Your Eyes, sleep now.

JOURNEY 17

Long rows of sectioned windows provide runway space for bounders, bugs and freedom's lure. Inside, classroom antics draw ire as a barrage of rubber bands slaps the panes. Antennae search for intruders, winged hoppers brace, stay.

The snicker of mischievous school boys, muffled by a slight touch of conscience, breaches the delicate hush of study time. Chalkboard pointer crashes with outrage, purposely close to offending shooters, to rival the soft roar of unleashed vocal fury of the substitute teacher. Clamor and classroom bedlam, calling card of an early friend, icon. Impishly funny, slightly irreverent, so engaging. Always leading, early dropout, wit and charm Dull To candid insurrection, desperate pleas. Early antics, chasing approval, fail to answer barren Hopes.

Punishing pain, once reserved for self, brim and overflow, Taking no captives, sparing no sympathies. Seeking only

JOURNEY 18

Shards of sunlight frozen in flight, chill grips the morning air as the solstice of winter fashions a splendid advent. Nature bows to its own weight, straining even the most robust of species. Bristling winds paralyze the frigid descent inciting a kaleidoscope of icy constellations. Merciless gods of tundra ignore impassioned pleas for reprieve in favor of a more eternal course. Perspectives of the day, shallow and arrogant, flake in the light of an unseen infinite wisdom. The glimmer of conventional regard pales in mirrored reflection as accumulating seasons chronicle truth irrefutable. Interpretations and conjecture flail, faulty since man's dawning. Fleeting parallel glimpses bear no perceptible evidence of nature's more excellent way. Only the frailty of man's vision comes under scrutiny- as vain inference falls at the foot of reason, timeless discernment begs the splice of ages'

JOURNEY 19

Playtime's twisted escapades rise to ravage the pretense of the huddled children. Unleashed demons dance in shadows of dread, seen through the patchwork of a quilt that surely had been tied for someone of favor. A quelled scream pierces only the essence of thought as the phantom hovers above us. Knowing that our first sound will bring certain Doom, breath escapes heavy chests, morose pitch gathers, shhhh. Don't move, don't breathe. Fifty cents an hour and this guardian of the day, paid to watch the kids while mom steps out. Just next door, just an hour or so, the unfinished basement room, and a surreal slashed. Intrusions on naivety, we trust, believe, and wait. Stillness broken, the door creaks, footsteps on the Stairs, the end is near. Circling with cloaked, deliberate footfall, Shimmering blade poised to descend at first quiver. First a snicker, a laugh and our cover is gone. For now, time to go, mom's home.

JOURNEY 20

Locker room mischief, a theater of pretense, myths of 'team spirit' and 'all for one'. Believing, wanting to belong, whatever it takes. Feigned clichés and the desire behind them, purge the Morals Of the one, willingly, in exchange for the right to win. Undefeated, proud, unbeatable in their league and Conviction, 'til the amusement wanes, and a more twisted course Takes shape. From a core of conceit, self-indulgence is worshiped, Weakness in others must be exposed, scorned, pinnacled for derision. Ambition personified, identified, caustic plan laid. Force the vulnerable link out, start with a little fear, Then a bruise, a jolt, no harm, just fun, this drama Intensifies. Conscious threats, jeers, shoves, pent up energy now violent, malicious, and hurtful. The unwary victim withers to the stinging blows, Searching and reaching, no tangible reason for being cast out there. The remaining half light slips with each new contact made, Groping for the door, the bench, slipping through, Crashing to the cold tile, friends…team…is there anybody to hear?…dark, thick Silence is the only sound remaining. Rusty showers trickles the echo of betrayal and cruel treachery, each escaping drop splinters, cools, brings senses back. Dull and distant recall invades the awakening, so cold, so wet, where could this place be? Sight slowly restored, faculties deny the verity of the vicious onslaught. The final wrenching, expulsion from the circle. "Why me", the muffled groan begs. Outside, the black of night recedes, early light struggles to offer hope or warmth. There is a cleansing in the air and a wish graces my lips, only to perish.

JOURNEY 21

Melancholy nightmares held captive in a pre- dawn Orb Speak to pensive withdrawal, unspoken dreams. The carnage of just intentions fall to dung heaps, teaming with the pungency of spoiled milk. Milk poured to ritualize the delight of fresh baked cookies, The revelers absent, conveniently slipping away. Sour and acerbic, ascribed flavors remaining when Failure grips And becomes what is real, what is remembered. What remains begs the inquiry, When conclusions are undeviating, where is this a Test? Despite years of novel and biased affirmation, pronounced defiled paths acquiesce to unchanging conclusions. Tribulation, trial, and other terms of affliction, Bear no sympathy, care not for the outcome, but sit placid as kings, infallible rulers. Pious, these eternal judges mete out grave disposition, As if their very existence mattered. So is this day, beleaguered, presupposed, expected, full of pits, and pity – marvel yet, nay, a mock Transformation, miraculous, The day, the immortal, the very infinite, the same.

JOURNEY 22

Lingering pains of time, years lapse, muffled utterances, filtered, yet amplified, recognize a familiar blemish, eager to taint, linger in

Wounds still bare. The talk, this time, reflect on events of the day innocent, small, without meaning, just to front impending slumber. The voices, the tones, gathering residues of despair As dust through the ducts, clogging, choking, suffocating. Night and the silent soliloquy of sleep echo in the shadows of this day, smothering the music. Music from defiant lyricists, played boldly and deliberately, To deaden, then permeate the void of love and life. This twisted replacement satisfies, pacifies, bestows serenity at last Notes, bending softly, disobey the confused life of Their giver, To find a home within the passions of the taker.

JOURNEY 23

Hues of winter, harsh and cold, catch and refract the tranquil pink of sunset eastward. The deep magenta of a velvet sky holds close the gathering dusk. Looking over the expanse of the allure of an inland Sea, long departed, Primitive creatures rise from the brush, looming, Stalking shadows of prey. Swirling billows of icy froth cap the monsters, transcending time, Defiant of the lifeless repose of the high desert. Mountain vista, distant and obscure in Silhouette, Enveloped by night, periphery to the nocturne sky. Surrounded by the warmth of a truck stop café, Consciousness invades the fantasy. Raspy laughter cajoles the flustered waitress, straining to appear unpremeditated, natural. George Jones pacifies the clamor With only the smooth intonation of a silver tongue. Truly, it is enough to sustain the hint of a smile, to know, to witness an ebbing moment, given to what may be so intrinsically fused to the primeval.

KARL HICKEN

JOURNEY 24

Paramount introspection, touching the essence, assimilating, sanctimonious. Finally piercing matter Irreverent, even brazen with
self-conscious absolution Searching for a verdict, not guilty. Arduous
and rigorous the witnesses come, each a portrayal of the clutter of
internal duality. Seeming futility, though essential, arms of glory
beckon, pangs of malice invite. Justice in the balance, choices tower,
precipitous. Ascending the cliffs, seeking not just a view, but the desperate glimpse of a companion, elusive. Flirting with the veneration
of fear, the edge looms invitingly close. Expecting the requiem of a
requite gaze from adjacent Vista. Apex cleared, the hope of finding,
but no, only sheerness of rock and knowing, there are no parallel
dementia, no fingertips to touch, just the behest of resilience, of a
rebirth or genesis, Solitary.

JOURNEY 25

Machiavellian vanity reflecting the ludicrous shadow of esteem Or
perhaps the void of such pretense. Can this shallowness of honor
create its own gulf of pride? The allowance of streams of internal
persecution, A desperate struggle of avoidance, hide first, then flee.
Layered doubt, the backdrop. Piercing criticism, administered in
droplets, 'til lathered as a thick shroud, suffocating the purity, the
natural.. Immersed and breathless, life flickers, wanes. Oddly predictable, strength gathered from weakness, Buoying the deflated soul.
Ominous hints of irrepressible anger, expressed in tones of sarcasm,
contempt. An audacious front conceals pain of seclusion before rip-
ening into a most bitter countenance. Justifying judicious, penance

granted, The sin becomes the sinner, a new stranger. Finally, a convincing, interment an assurance, an All is well, Oh God, have mercy.

JOURNEY 26

Moonlit lyrics inspired from sleepless dreams, and I believed in love. I knew one day you would grace me, recognize my hollows, overwhelm my senses, permeate my shallow veneer, measure my heart. That, then, the rhythm of two might give meaning To the drumming of one. Through ingenuous eyes, truth touches light, Ephemeral hopes petition conviction from the eternal. Ageless pursuit of life, a place, consumes, feels, perhaps, like love should. Perhaps, defined in nearness, in flesh, in rich velour of thot, your presence is home, relaxed. Mesmerized with desire, hope, illusion, charmed images take shape as a symphony of tranquility. The harmonizing of colors, as the strands of a rainbow, intertwining as two, impassioned as one, recline impervious to anything else. Coveting, your gifts find vacancy in my soul and the tenement halls breathe new life. Do I thank you or bid you clemency? Your kindness, diligence, and willingness are the instruments of orchestral wholeness. I know I shall never deserve you, In solemn awe, I reverence your gifts to me. My conscious reality leaves so much empty for you. Tender mercies beseeched, I love you.

JOURNEY 27

Lifelines, durable and painstakingly fabricated, Strewn between those alive and those that live. To live is to reminisce in the passion of the

Evocative, To inhale the essence of one's sigh, then forge the union of desire and choice. Capture the will, the fire of the one who lives and incendiary delights inwardly warm the master. Fruition flatters magnanimous, overstatement, resides confirms to the willing observer, seeking such, just a teardrop, you to me, and I too may live. Those alive, worship the gods of drudgery, batter and blame the blemish of their existence. Intrinsic and concentric, the gravity of self contrition Begets inertia, kinetic by privilege, enervated by preference. Taut and sure lines of life voluntarily passed on, scoffed at, Saves no one blinded by such folly. 'Tis as a kiss on the lips of the dead, aspiration gone limpid, silenced with impunity. Keep your teardrop, your repressible dearth, I favor life.

JOURNEY 28

Hushed and honored as familiar spirits enter, eyes so long blind stir and welcome the long since departed. Exquisite peace permeates, transforms us, grandma and me. Her whispered utterance, "Karl you're here", and I am filled with him. Myth and veil melted, another joins, "I know you, I trust you, stay, please". Dane, sweet, pure, guardian, soul mate, genteel angel, pauses to touch me, grandma smiles. Having tasted this moment, residues of lucidity Lingering, spiritual belonging, no pretense, nothing spurious, Just tranquility. Empty spaces, voids brim with euphoric Residence, an eternal circle fused, frozen in an absence of time. Psalms of serenity speak to each present, intense stillness conveys thought, without Words. From these lips and life, parched and worn, shadows of sin flee, forgiveness reigns, enraptured, prepared, grandpa extends a finger, to caress grandma's last breath.

"Good-bye, uncommon friend", escapes my tongue, as the angelic procession gathers their beloved. A last squeeze, her hand in mine, withering flesh alone, devoid of spirit, reposes, and the scars of mortality are quieted. Evidence of divinity sheathes the now empty room.

Bowing my head in serene reverie, I am graced by this blood and this life, illuminated privileged. And transfigured, presence This farewell, etched in contrasts, for me, a promise left, a memory forever moored.

JOURNEY 29

Seems as though all personal dichotomy Is recorded in monotone. Legions of scenes fraught with clear and silent Deception justifying the middle Without Opposition. Sort takes the edge off of assigning fault, When harmony has no lines, no sides to take, And well learned lessons speak to the need To maintain a perilous perch. Psychotic lesions drain the lifeblood Of a balance prescribed by order, Dictated by self appointed icons of communion. Utterances invade desecrated shrines and bunkers of meditation fall. Yet the gentle wrath of a heartless parody sanctions the abandoned silence, vindicates the mortar of voiceless halls. Must write, must pen and must I really pretend to subscribe to the nothingness of hollow theory. Honoraria dispensed from wall hangings, mete with the drunken mutterings of the inane. Holding on, faith, hope fades to what is paltry, healing, yes, healing, hoist a toast, the hometown leads the game, and healing, means what to me.

JOURNEY 30

Why are you running away? Just the thought that there may be somewhere to run

To.

So unknown, the destination of the final escape. Encumbered in lore, heavens gate draws fear, a mirage, mirrored on pools of Satan's heavy breath. Mystical theories package this place, extolling guilt, hailing a more excellent lie. No place to play, outside, too dank, stifling, inside, there is no room, no time. Convergent worlds consume light, gravity, in a triggered rush to carnal Armageddon. Shadows fill the empty spaces, once vacated, nomads of dignity lost. Prescience sought, even second sight, companions behind a cryptic curtain. Illusion, euphoria, reality hazed, each allies of preferred company, conspirators. There is no running away. Empty still. By choice?

Absent.

JOURNEY 31

Silent, stealthful, slow, sure. Puhleeeze, love at home is a trigger. The guise, the beauty, the result? Envy, ensuing killer, inside rotting out.. Obsessed with the trappings of all the other's lives. Is it fame, is it to have, or to hold? Is it a smile on the face of the pathetic? The promontory of self-derision stalks the source, the Cradle. Did I do this... to me? Do I still?

Surely there is a pathway to the ethereal retreat. Maybe a stage more giving than the player. A format for voices, deceived and searching. Must be a plank to walk, a balance, precarious. Material losers jealous of the travesty sulk in a pool of lifeless impotence. Tell me of happy faces with the

Glossy magazine countenance, Fronted with a grin, balanced on a narrow beam, Must be something in it for them. Finally, a wish I wish. Freedom from the need to judge, to dispense judgment. To gnaw at the fiber of someone else's sincerity. To see the finish, unmarred, beautiful. To leave what is well and fair alone. To give just to give, knowing motive to be pure, without rancor. To bid latent exoneration and allow such a wish residence.

JOURNEY 32

Everything to gain?

Everything to gain…

What have we to give?

Probing, scouring, inhaling the infinite truth, knowing the nothingness of human offering. Vicarious at best, yet hollow recesses plead irresolute. No gift, no proffering manifest. Only a spiraling, humbling descent. Is it pure, can the leverage span the rift? Unsteady motives, transparent rationalizations breach the cause, sever the well intentioned. Bartering with eternal reasoning, wants and needs blur to skew the simplicity.

Duplicitous mortality, belonging Craving Celestial Reach for the bliss, fingertips brush, parched lips Imagine the sweetness of the nectar. Nectar, healing balm, the Great equalizer. Weep for us, pure tears, immaculate ointment. Sufficient to the day, this unrefined gratuity, placed at the feet of the giver, miracles visited, covenants renewed.

JOURNEY 33

Downtown, bus stop, Woolworth's soda fountain. Just four of us, eyeing the scene, plotting, uh huh, Plan conceived. Memories to be made, friendships to challenge. Allegiances will today be summoned, tried. Mischief emerges coupled as right, wrong, who knows? Free kid show ended an hour ago, #5/19th east bus runs on the half 'til nine. Time so idle, a saint would find trouble, and we could use a dose. Table set, strategy defined, intelligence gathered. This slick machine, yes us, rogues of disorder make a play, sugar packets, all of them. Systematically, counter holders are swept into the plot, then returned, restored, as little soldiers guarding empty bunkers. Sweet booty fills the pouches of hooded sweats, spilling at the seams. So smooth, so cool, we hum a bar of nothing, and walk unscathed. Out, undetected, unfettered, Summer sun softens the asphalt street. Curbside, watching, the grooves of bus tires sink before rolling away into the mirage of exhaust, musing.

Dirty water picks a path along my curb, my gutter, Scurrying, as if to out run itself. Aha, I shall sweeten the flow, Liberate a captive packet, now, maybe not. Through the azure haze of smoke and heat Comes our Bus, stagnant pools now fill the pocks of the gutters, stilled. New games to play, we scramble to the back of the Empty bus. Setting a command center, discipline bows out, accepting. Stop after stop, sugar scrappers rule, until…wait! Hesitant, unsure mercenaries regroup for the offensive. The spoils of the clash, sticky and scattered, fill the furrows, the runners, at the rear of the bus. Senses sharp, we know, the real trouble is heading our way. Last stop, end of the line, "Yes, sir, Mr. Driver" "We saw the whole thing, but… we don't know 'em".

JOURNEY 34

The sting of wind whipped sand… Punishment for a wish out of season. Spring squall fills the horizon, heavy rolling quilted nimbus lumbers through the basin, threatening. Staircase of eons plays host to the presence of the maleficent storm.

'You are here' captures the thought,

A blessed gift beheld, considered. The grace of a teary smile in this parched Eden seals what the National Parks gingerly scores at the markers. Another gust splashes my face restores conscious awareness- Startled by the sheer majesty of the walls of magenta stone, breath escapes with the bluster, to become one with forces of creation. The awe, the rush of inhaling the grandeur, draws strength, confuses meaning, the shudder consumes, is it fear, or the hallowed hush of heaven's nearness?

JOURNEY 35

A note on a queued score, a smear of pigment splashed on parchment, a single utterance on the ears of the impassioned… To touch the ethereal plane. Lifting the spirit, immortalizing the secret winds, Soaring on wings of an author unknown, only felt, in the folds of dreams. This place, this ray of zealous warmth, sought, only to fringe, never to enter fully, reside. To softly rap at the gate,

To plead and stretch, strain. I know you, not the person, but the persona, take me with you. And I am taken by you, to become the wings, the breath beneath. The sweet scent of the nocturne sky carrying the trades of the climes, pales to you. A quiver, a gentle soul shudder, heights unrivaled, not recognized, known. This kiss, this love affair of words, the lips that utter, Enchantment.

Euphoria.

Pleasure.

Elation.

Bliss.

JOURNEY 36

Lest the stranger is an angel, adolescence mocks the thought. May I find the portal to me in them? Cliques and clichés, makeup, masking the self inflicted soul crippling.

'Find me, rescue me, hold me', importunes the gentle voice, inaudible. Look... Not at me, stupid, through me. My eyes, go ahead, don't listen to my tone, I beckon your gaze, please.

The spiraling passage, gateway, my eyes. Hazed, clear, no matter, I flee your probing, hide, still hoping to be found. Others have been here, surface intentions exposed, lies, wrapped, scented, I cannot bear the insult, another false witness borne. Listen?

Deafness screams to eavesdrop, keep you away. There is light, so faint... Don't run, I feel it, too. I know you, recognize the flicker, Feel what you feel, wait here. So faint, imperceptible, traces of love, mocked now, by care givers, captured in pretense, obligation. We touch in this domain, I believe you. I want to trust you. I wear the riddled baggage, apparel of the accused, the accursed. Pure and sweet, this essence of spirit, this fallen angel, stranger, wanderer, seeking consolation, acceptance, 'Hey Mister, do you have the time?

JOURNEY 37

Oklahoma City, safe, warm spring days underemployment totally overwhelming my preoccupation. Glistening pools of last night's rain fill the yard swing, Rivers of moss drip over the planks into the abyss of the dark world under the deck. Atop the gazebo, tiny, vigorous droplets race to form patterns of paratroopers, anxious, nervous vaults.

Tranquility, and the very rays of the April sun, so placid and serene breached by the advent of evil, premeditated and salacious. So slight, scarcely a quiver, the ominous truth suffered by each pane. Arrested into instant timelessness, the dance of the après shower surrenders, the upward tropism of fresh flowers rescinds to an unthinkable act of God's crown creation. The wrath of hate, jealousy...but,

Why the children, so fragile, without defense, without malice, again, why the children? The angst of mothers, stripped of a life borne willingly, To fulfill their measure. Fathers bent to provide a finer life, dreaming dreams, little leaguers, tea parties, sweetest of parental visions. The sweat of honest work, the aspirations of epochs, The hopes of a generation now altered. Zealous media eager to air the laundry, horrify the world and the soul with images of war-torn Middle America, and we feel our own pulse, waning, Paralyzed with the lifeless innocence.

Each of us was there, inhaling the voracious evil, choking, suffocating, engorged in the flames of Hell. Every knee bowed, every heartstring grasped for a next beat, And finally, it came, venerated. For a moment, hate and envy swallowed, the most bitter of rivals bowed, divergent philosophies mingled, the relentless right to win relinquished its celebrated zenith to don the gauntlet of compassion. From the glass, shattered on the library floor to the twisted wreckage that identified a life of belongings of the homeless, none went unattended. Cradled by the merciful hands of temporary angels, Humankind judgment. Rendered service, without Radiant, glorious heroes, common folks, uncommonly united departed the provincial for a sacred vigil of relief.

A sojourn from Gomorrah to Gethsemane, compelled the survivors, each of us, in our living rooms, or succoring a friend, to a more tender outreach and forgiveness. Statistics staggering our very being, undeniable, irrevocable, unconscionable. Yet the breath that utters, "This cannot happen ever again", deceives no one, nor changes the course of Events.

The lone peaceable walk, each step, so individual and interpolative, are we willing? The gait of the willing, ensuing the tear of the new found righteous, captures the sigh of a generation. We must embrace the wonder, pursue the path of reconciliation, affirm and believe in each other. Oklahoma city, spring still blooms, still safe, still warm in me.

JOURNEY 38

Sugar House Park, semblance of serenity, irreverent cradle of a generation of rebellion, entangles me in desire.

Oh, how my Dad hated the sojourn to the upper ball

Fields, 25 m.p.h. through the curves, round the pond, VW buses rockin' with long hairs. Sweet, bitter wafts of smoky insurrection invades the virtues of the uninvited. T'was the meeting of Ms. Pamela that holds this place I believed in her freedom, craved her expressions. I watched as she danced, so unbridled. Her flame licked at my innocence, as the earth allowed her space to glide over its surface. Barefoot, adorned in nature, fantasy's embodiment. Secluded qualm, so intense, and I shrink, she's looking at me, for me.

I yearn for this, melt my insignificance, please, don't stop, Ms. Pamela, I want this dance. Free flowing, her lusty drape, enshrouds her, now me in timeless giving. To leave the boundaries, and accept a gift, can it be for me? Moments measured, right, wrong?

JOURNEY 39

Solace in oblique numbness, divorcement of self to the wounds that lock out, vacuous conscious energies reap havoc. Agony escapes to apathy, pleasure's tollgate refusing entrance, secluded forbidden relations, wearing the mask of the mirrored. Spurious incantations escape the youthful tongue, sleeved, disguised, packaged, silenced. Serenading, the lone dancer plays host to an empty ballroom. Shades drawn to dim the entanglement encompassing sinew and soul, yet, wholeness fills and threatens renewal. This cotillion, the masquerade, visited and revisited, impassioned, so vivid, plays to the whispers of the very marrow. Testing the fibers of such a being, the gods weave wings of healing, pillowing, cradling… shhhh… listen… repose.

JOURNEY 40

Masters of passion, then and now, to move what is felt, I am compelled by the pilgrimage.

To release, to please, just to appease the magnitude of the unquenchable, coveted fusion. The chasms loom so large, breaking thru the vortex, inexorable. Must be a latent radiance, buried 'Neath the rubble of sanctioned garbage. Tired remains of useless energy squandered, dormant, somnolent, waiting. The fuse is lit, no one runs, blanketed intensity runs fever pitched, swelling with each expression quilled. Bursting to be something, someone, there is no measurement, no reckoning of time, just the sheer ecstasy of sharing. Of connecting, planning, spiraling, touching, loving the heights of breaking free. No more glibly paying homage to the "Supposed to be's."

JOURNEY 41

A world away from a most frenzied metropolis, off of a sandbar, a veritable long island, there is a serene hunt ensuing.

The treasure is worthless, but to the collector, who combs the sand with fine tooth toes, each piece has meaning, history. East coast sea glass, dubious in origin,

Remnants of a careless society, castaways from years of dumping, swept by tides, lap at the northern shore. Virtuosos at the vigil appear, legendary in the art,

With tales of lore, intrigued with the colors. Smooth and lustrous, years of finish catalog the worth of each find. To fill the display jar, therein is the treasure, layers of history distinguished in rare pigments. Though uncommon in individual stature, all concur To play this game, one must find the blues.

JOURNEY 42

The ocean sun, obsequious, unassuming in noon day

Brilliance,

Warms and serves the worshipers in their sacred vigil.

As if naturally, the daily climb goes on, cresting the blue horizon, challenging the deep hues of the water at the apex,

Climaxing as the waning spoils of the day suspend and transform what has no equal into the magic of sunset.

Unparalleled shades of evening blur obscurely into an eternal curtain call. Perspectives clear, laughter permeates, I'm blessed to find the same smile today that allowed the briny mist to surrender its position and moisten my cheek. T'was a birthday, after all, my first born accepted three years same as an eventual nineteen, twenty, twenty one... The zeal of timeless waves lapped onto our feet, old, young, same. Sunset, seething with majesty, vexatious with mood, suspended in atmosphere, having spent its course, relinquished the stage.

Warmth grows as the vibrancy of dusk reigns, kindled by a bright eyed birthday wish. Twilight, splendor incarnate, breathe deeply the luster. Streaks of vivid corals splash the deepening 'Tis a proper moment playing host to suitable rites, Reverberating, sitting cross-legged, spanning intangibles, content

JOURNEY 43

This day starts ok, the sun's orthodox disappearing act vilifies the cruel paradox of Sunday. Ahhhhh, the day of rest, the very Sabbath, set aside, hallowed, sanctified. Sanctimonious moments that sway the balance, pharisaical masters supplicate, 'Look at me.' Entreated at the gates, I enter, heavy with judgment, crimson with contempt. Cautious to offer the hand of fellowship, the dilemma deepens, the shallow greetings flow superfluously, then race down the drain, with and to be with the runoff of nature. Sanctuary of the saints, cold statuaries stare from their pews. Hallways bend, jagged obstacles strewn to hinder the view, the path to the straight and true.

Oozing with the wisdom of a terrier in heat, the conversations repulse with the monotones of the familiar. Unable to silence the din, disillusioned hysteria retreats, Delirium abandoned, in search of a less caustic fervor. Quite sure that this noise is my own, the hardness breaks, tolerance peeks in to disperse the webs of hate. Swept away, back under the rug, yet peering out, not disappearing, nor removed, just a day of rest.

JOURNEY 44

Softly indulgent, symphonies of thought, brushed with velvet strokes onto the canvas of the soul. Immersed in the solitude of a resounding score, each note a shiver, each strain an echo undulating. Billowing, swelling, bursting onto a floodplain of desire,

Each parched sensory receptor melting into the richness. Basking in the glow of the author's very image, inspiration melds into artistry. To pen the mellifluous aspirations Captivates this medium of expression. These modest words, so inadequate, pay mere perfunctory veneration, without exquisite instrumentation. Howbeit, may this humble offering of verse, with design to mesmerize and inspire, ignite the fiery blaze of passion, gently impart, and finally seduce.

JOURNEY 45

I quit.

When the familiar has no life, I quit. When life has forsaken the familiar, I quit. When irony comes to mutual agreement, challenging the plight of meritorious dissension, I quit. As trust reeks of the stench of the sump, I quit.

When I call and the receiver deceives me, I want to leave. If there is a bottom, I just don't want to be here. Where there is intangible peace, I shun, doubt. Holding to the dark pleasure of antagonism Becomes the glimmering horizon. Agonizingly human, frivolous love songs beckon this seemly departure. Oh, if only inmost wishes could change the permanence that hope neglects. When deity denies the knock, the disparate plea, then there is but one savior. Dissembled faith, tarnished and stained with contradiction, Impoverish and enervate what may have been saved. But, to quit, I welcome the envoy.

JOURNEY 46

In a place where post twilight's work is dream catching, temptation has not a place, but a home. Night rituals, fanciful fantasies worshiped, recognized as nocturnal idols of lust. Sought after musings of daylight, adjudged, accursed, sins imagined, never committed, simply desired. Soft pillows to cradle the weight, sleep laden eyes rhapsodize what may have been, or what may never be again.

The sting of life's reality, daily reminders by and from the well intentioned, bubbling in their own cauldron of guilt.

The rights, the wrongs, the strife of choices, turn away, immerse the offense, savor the secret wish.

Surreptitious meanderings, flights clandestine genius, trespasses avoided, introspectively revealed, run, find, fade into the escapade, the soliloquy of slumber. Of

So is the dream state, priceless, harmless, refuge and shelter from the tempests.

JOURNEY 47

A lyrical pinprick, the satiny flight of a butterfly, I yearn to feel the sounds, commiserate in the texture.

Must be a language of touch, pure symbols of thot, Inscribed on heartstrings.

Surreal alphabet, iconoclastic litanies, where origins of noise or overture of sight tingle each resonant sense.

Shrill intonations liberate reverberations, previously inaudible.

Tucked away sound, fragrance, touch, await extra sensory enlightenment. Sometimes a palpation, a fleeting glimpse, chased, to be lost, in a vapor of apparition. Worthy of the pursuit, not willing to relinquish, I search, listen, ponder the phrases unsung. Then, we will revel in this grammar, come closer, behold the genesis, yes, I feel it, too.

JOURNEY 48

So comfy, strained and pureed,

Mashed potatoes without lumps,

Buicks, generic remakes of Beatles classics. Adventures to challenge the medium to a more even mediocrity. Where the heights of peril and the risk of a fall rival drowning in an empty bath. The curse of being prosaic blesses the middle. Desirous to be burdened so aptly, endeavors of the average covet the prize, sort of. Pleasing to the masses, a place to make a mark simple, like fireworks with out a spark.

JOURNEY 49

Resurrection, the boy with the man, the pathway lengthens at each stride. There must be a way, an atonement, suffered by the man, sought by the boy. Intercessory conveyance, as the quaking of a falling aspen leaf, falls to the breath behind a canyon gust. The boy, entombed in a crucible of vacancy, bartered early a jealous heart for a silent pump, a fair swap, the childhood for a mask, the blues of summer skies for sightless gray. Wanton desertion to rule the day, tearful absence to govern the night, barely distinguishable betwixt. The man, captive to the consumption of life's offering,

Scorned repeated sightings of the boy. Blanked from existence, blindness led the man, to malign his own slight existence. A trace, imperceptible, the façade breached, increasing evidence of survival, The travail of a generation begs a common voice.

Can this divorcement be annulled?

The chilling insurrection now seeking a union, a restoration, a healing. Destitute, splintered and worn, the schism looms unsurpassable. Finally, have the strengths of the two exceeded the needs of the one?

JOURNEY 50

Reflections surround me, emotions soar. Expressions and memories, mirrored in words of reality and hope... Venturing back, early drama, seeking approval, I see the world of this child.

Driven to be, yet without direction. Outside life's vistas change, it's not all bad. Change is predictable, even stable. Young and strong, the years as days, our firstborn finds his way... Guideposts, we are, sentinels, markers, at times silent, pointing. Pulling and pushing, challenging the child. Defining a role, significant, yet destined to fade. As time reveals the boy to himself, thinking that I should make a difference. For him, I smile, today, I thank God for choices, some by consent, others divine. Gracing us, the child and the dad, a tribute to a choice, the one we call Mom. Self sacrificing and nurturing, worried, unjustly guilty, appropriate, sincere, purposefully dedicated...

A little moody, complex, fiercely loyal, to us, and we, barely notice, on the surface. Heart's treasures are stored, wisdom matures. It is not for me to be the difference, but to partake, blessed by both. Youthful and passionate now… this season. Music, philosophy, and the origin of dreams. Compelled and compelling, we follow the energy of Creation. Threads of glory bound together, strong and resolute. Agency and Priesthood, profoundly empty without Man.

Tears of angels bear record to the waves and tides of humanity committed to deny. The right to choose now, to fulfill the full measure of life on earth… The majesty of sunrise, the deep blues of sunset pale in comparison to God's promises, if we but choose to act. The season, the time, the right to dream dreams, are for most but a passage, an entitlement of sorts. Wasted and lost, age, not wisdom, triumphant. Wishes… languishing in the surreal are not the stuff of dreams or of this dreamer.

JOURNEY 51

Deeds and covenants, proof of what is whose, of whom is whose, why?

Time's frontiers, daily evolution, relationships, promises and vows… Borders established, minimums defined, Contradictions nurtured.

Choking in the mire of prolonged decline, Rights of soul ownership beg review.

Who owns me? Who would want to?

The present, the future, a bank? Spare me.

A friend, a lover, a certificate of marriage?

A clock, a time clock?

Who really can make the past live?

The past, Hmmmm, could be. When possession becomes procession, heavy with cadence, lines drawn, measured. Hot tip! Hostage situation, no negotiators, bright with friends, seeking what? Nets of wonder, secret ambitions, inner tides swelling with resins, demeanors lacerate, bleed, clutch for gain. Codes, legitimately crafted, serve the artisan, bind the parties, but matters transform. Who serves what, time or needs, needs conflict. Maybe it is time. Yes, it's time.

JOURNEY 52

Good brother, you spoke well today, yourself, your lovely family. Your years of being away, you wear well enough. Dear friend, ecclesiastical forerunner, I caught in your gaze, a caring unfamiliar.

You needn't find room for me anymore, your significance sustains us both. You, of the present order, tend your flock, just nod if I'm still here. Oh, glad to see me, but you didn't, no, no, please, tend your flock. Compassionate, gentle wonder, there are gifts much finer than I have bathed your feet in. You are the foundation of such greatness, I remain in your awe, distantly.

To the era of my youth, life, tolerance, the peculiar wisdom I shoulder, forgive my generational breach, reparations are for the gods to hallow. A toast to the angels, a kiss to a guardian an expanse, without confines, lays open before me.

Granted tender mercies as seem fit, this glass darkly may shed a light.

JOURNEY 53

Is what's right wrong in me? Royal birth, chosen generation. Children of promise falling short. Exposed to quasi-devout whips and chains, and a bondage of righteous caretakers. Vigils, ceremonial rebirth, the memory of conscious forgetting. Celebration of gifts, confused, distorted, misdirected. Meant for me? Lost to others. Rites of maturing, select bestowals conferred on a void of preference.

Mantle endowed, commitment confirmed, but, oh, the pain of questions, unanswered. Don't ask, don't suspect, right is right. Doubt not the dubious faith of the believer. Emerging duplicity, espouse the genre du jour. Ignore the tempest of dawning rage, favor a path umbrellas' from the talons of adversarial predators. Straight and narrow, the course. So obvious, no one dies there. Forces beyond and within the natural overrule suppression to validate the normal. Choice, the elocution of desire, the articulation of the soul,

Search for the peaceable stride,

Finally letting wrong find right in me.

JOURNEY 54

A gentle swell; a curious urge, cresting the curl; a pinprick drawing blood crashing, pounding, retreat denied; entangled in the maelstrom. Pressures of the tide; tied to the persuasion, inhaling the exhilaration of the zenith; justifying the worth of the addiction. A few bucks; a flirtatious tryst, willing, wanting an edge; the sweet savor of a forbidden kiss a life's savings; beyond rescuing a breath, faulty loans, untimely summons; inexorable desire, craving irreparable damage, panacea; fixation exceeded, nirvana gained. Nothing measured next to the compulsion, irrational costs; indispensable worth. Levy the pursuer, avail the partaker. Obsession, god of the impassioned mortal, justifies the pleas, chases the storms, cherished pleasure, buried pain, listen, it's a madman.

JOURNEY 55

"Choose me," echoes the chant, as sides are divvied up for kick soccer. Fingers crossed for no one to see I close my eyes and hope. "Pick me," pretty school girl, and the bus lurches forward belching a plume of black smoke. She passes, I blush and hope. "Take me," slips the whisper, and the hush of the chilling breeze answers as the boisterous car full of ski friends embraces the bluster.

Taillights abate, disappear, I recoil in the snow and Hope. "Marry me," a gilded voice beckons the vow.

The forage for love's enchantment persuades the blind eye and yes, it is done.

Now I shrink with impunity and hope drifts.

"Find me," somewhere strewn in life's moraine. The verdancy of spring, the harshness of summer,

To the withering of autumn. Winter's glacial heart trickles veins of arrested hope.

"Forget me," better still. A smile casually drifts across my face, almost stunning, almost revealing.

"Choose me, please."

JOURNEY 56

Jealousy, common fury spearing necessary simplicity.

Sensitivities, veritable throbbing of the heart upset by flagrant innuendo, unintended oblation.

Where is motive? What is to gain? Is there purpose?

The burden of misguided feeling conjured, the useless energy of presumption squandered. One-sided tears shed over reality perceived, reality denied.

There is no host, no hostess, no reason, no signs, only sighs frittered away, when barely breath or tears are wasted.

An enigma, without form, spewed from within. Insane cravings, driven belief in a withering rose.

Just out there, scarce a base, uncomfortable, so insecure, crying for substance untouched, unspoiled.

Truth? Warranted lies to feel better...

Sad to one day discover, there is no spoil, no soiled threads in the fabric tho tarnished with life stains, tainting, defiling stains, and hues change. Storybook purity, blurred illustrations, faded inks all blur to the musing touch. So many unauthorized alterations, never authored, never altered.

JOURNEY 57

Stop the show, my scenes are over. No, don't stop, departure is imminent. Drawn to a mystical world buried, sequestered, silently inviting. Immersed in the glossies of the Geographic,

Fingers of thot claw thru the millennia.

Temples and serpents that coexist to rule the jungle know me, spirits of the ancients draw me,

As though familiar.

Forest and citadel align as a peaceable abutment, one giving as the other takes, knowing secrets are safely tucked away.

The cresting of the tropical sun, slivers of radiance, burst onto the beach, still warm from yesterday's alliance.

The tiara of each footprint, florescent from gathered moon streams shared, delight as gentle breezes perfect each tenet.

Gentle shafts of purest sunlight, bend to grace the cool of the shadows. Swells of the tide, heaving, surging, hold tight to each shimmering, luminous peak, then break, releasing a fury of sun drenched passion.

The corals of endless sands revere each passing wave, still. "One way, please."

"What's that? Thank you, but no."

"Pardon me, I missed what you just said."

"Ah yes, business, and yes, so personal."

"Have I excess baggage?

All I am carrying is superfluous now, you keep it here."

JOURNEY 58

Answer the call of the curious,

Tempt the hollow deafness of the bizarre. Legions lead the cry, piercing demons dance to the inquisitor. Tattered, shredded saviors adorn the mind ways, kiss the fervor guarding the portals to terror. Dark lullabies lumber with lechery, groaning low to be heard, for an audience to delude.

Each tone strikes with adolescent tampering imparting the apparition's breath. Hues, thick and dense with evil, against a backdrop of sheer translucence mirror reflections of self, and private fears. Strip the secluded nakedness, expose the recessed carnality, dread the realization, abhor the imperiled. Fear, the very shuddering of, the trembling heart of which, tacitly stalks the core, grips each victim, in its innocence.

Haughty contenders, seeking to better the score, quip with evil's wreath, wear the scourge, live to die.

JOURNEY 59

Chasing to mollify the familiar, sedation is a friend. Demeaning conversation the alliance of cognizant Strikes a precedence, takes an earned place. Clinging to the murk of ante sleep pondering, Fading consciousness curses, lifeblood courses. Diametric designs polarize emotions, responses lag,

And the traveler occurs.

Without the means to identify, what seems so real fails to arrive at significance. What is good enough to take down, seeks such a descending level, as to add, or even make comfortable. Dense light bearing tribute, presenting lucid amulets for the damned, alms given, seized, never given, borne by the poor.

You follow the path of the cheery, covert deceptions. Cover the contradiction, make it not be so. Deny the voyage, choose your form, enter with resolve, reign in unity, guarded.

JOURNEY 60

I know my toaster

I believe the plans of my toaster to be secretly guarding a number, a secret. I know that a push button window, electrical marvels that they are, will go over that digit in a dirty wind. I see the architects of age, this age, clandestine in design to build in numerological obscurity. I wonder, sardonically, is a universal smile monitor, waiting to flip my switch, quiet my smile? I know this heart.

I know that somewhere there is a number. Maybe I hold that number.

JOURNEY 61

Blueprints detailing the choices, everlasting, equivocate the masses. Foundations of disassembly breach, then honor shallow thought.

Walls, hollow, constructed without scruples, rot from within. Conditional morals extol the integrals, just to test the fibers.

Situational ethics canonize the generations. It's not new, it's not old, it's not clever, not ever. But conclusions are true to time, always.

Materiality in disarray, pride becomes the pinnacle, not just the stuff, anymore. Bigger, bolder prizewinner, still unscathed, unfettered.

Hmmm… wonder how they do that.

JOURNEY 62

Seasons cascading over the peaks, Capturing and absorbing all,

Trickles through the bluing mist of the scrub oak. There must be exhilaration, inhaled

Alive, giving life to the inanimate. Praises sprinkled as each evening ray\ in the grandeur, pure, vigorous, calm. Reach out of the dreary doldrums of what entraps the soul. There is a summons in the natural, a link inseparable. This chapel is tranquil in twilight, yet the silence is not emptiness, contrary, 'tis full of its own companionship. This vestry, brimming with lively musicians escape the view of the streaming congregations, only to be truly adored in the collaborative.

Of choices, pretended, or executed, Life beams, brilliant, radiant, craving for audience

Most unclaimed, fall as the fill of commitment devours sentient reflection.

JOURNEY 63

The cool breeze of a May evening barely stirs, yet clouds in cadence are brisk in passing. Resolute moon rules the passage, Not yet full, ancient cries ascend and reverberate,

Petition the winds and grow strong,

Nourished by the Mother. High desert birds, nervous messengers

Overhead, voices yet to be stifled by withering heat ahead.

Valley of goblins, hoodoos and shadows, Ostentatious, pompous, stage is set, games begin. Each could be the hider,

Each could be the seeker. Air, crisp and tart, silently gasping, to avoid being found, especially first. Dad's easy, they say, not this time, It's just me and my commune, stars, moon, my excellent hiding place, then willingly,

A sigh to be heard, a giggle and Pop's "it," again.

JOURNEY 64

Deep, oppressive heat greets the fiery sunrise, craggy peaks gather the intensity, cradle the basin.

Verdant river vistas argue without avail, plead for place, settle for knowledge of time.

Incredible harmonies negotiated well before human eyes judged the majesty. Epochs without judgment, created, destroyed, left alone.

Hostile forces gentle and guided, twist and turn, carve and combine, to span the incomparable moment, repose, then vacate to seem tranquil, serene. Pleasures of brilliance, dawn comes breaking, rules the morn, warms the bones. Treasures of timeless toil, inanimate labor force, create, then captured in a moment, still, what we, proud architects of progress, covet.

The fire belongs here, the peaks, the vistas, the basin, the knowledge of time.

Inimitable. Belonging. Untamed.

JOURNEY 65

Gods of leisure river of tail lights as in a downpour a flash flood of anxious road rampage to beat the next to worship at a wilderness throne to kneel at the trolling alter quintessential pilgrimage to the sacred sites hookups burnt offerings trumped lies to establish rule of the liars not just the lies but how big how many to brag of the misery of weather tantrums equipment that rarely works the ones that got away, again And this is always new always bigger, better, drunker more indulgent higher sacrifices required

By gods without sense or senses humor or forgiveness. Whew!!!

JOURNEY 66

Siblings, cheeks pressed to the pane, horrified, at what may be. Mom's left, the grinding plate of frustration, angst, so fused to the blade, snapped, shattered, and now, Mom's gone. The eyes of the unblemished watch, the fingers that need her touch, reach, held back by the glass.

This matronly departure, dark winter long coat, an icy, wintry road, a faded scarf around locks of gray, Her eyes, heavy in her own tears, never look back.

I know she'll come home.

She always does. We'll promise to never, ever, do this again.

I trust the promise, but know me. From the corner, where hearth brick intersects the big room, consternation fills my head. Shrinking, so small, as not to be seen, achieved insignificance eases guilt.

You just think you see me. I can make you go away, too. Uh huh, I saw her coming up the walk. Maybe if I didn't talk, anymore. "I'll try once more, if you will."

JOURNEY 67

Enter at the door, try to predict guess who today, stupid toothbrush, it has no meaning, honest, I don't know why you-So, why you?

Just your turn Not sure I can stand that expression the vacancy, the simplicity the vacuous chambers. Shall I tell you something? How about a simple tease? You wouldn't get it. Then the pain I would have to bear to be forced to continue. Look at me, Come over here.

That's you in the mirror. Bedtime has come, there is no one to save, watch, you really can't see me, can you? Sure, stand here, careful, the face in the mirror the eyes of the silent rage stalk the opportunity to hurt.

There is no target person, only the will to hurt, help me to satisfy the need. The crashing glass fills the sink Foaming toothpaste spit spills up onto the broken pieces… Breathe it, timeless, stillness, euphoric numbness engulfing, and for the moment the sickness subsides.

Darting, shooting terror has come now to fill what was so imperceptible. There, isn't some emotion more challenging than the emptiness of none? All of you look to me, at me for reason, for theological reconnection. Tell her you're sorry, tell her or else. The door has a closer as well find it, use it, get lost.

Write a resolution, a new creed, call someone who for a moment has a charge to pay preoccupied attention. You speak of love, you tell me of choice, you even cry on my old cheap shirt, warn me of the blood and sin of a generation, my generation.

These hollow breaches of intelligence are contemporary, yes? So, exonerate the universal, break through, just once, please. One real, verifiable, knock down, drag out, believable, without excuse effort. I know it's my turn to go with you. Are there new stories? Does your way have space for mine? Or, is there still only guilty rhetoric? Buy me a double cheese, at the Red Steer then, yes, we'll go, and this one, too, I tuck with the others…

JOURNEY 68

Retention of direction, is this a malady of discontent?

The dichotomy of dilemma and focus is lost to a frenzied blur. To judge and pursue, falls to pressure of bi-polar demands.

Be content to view the enigma outside in. Paradigms of unequal latitudes barely shift, twixt the choices. Inside, the brutal and the exhilarant, the lovely and the abominable bunk in confined chambers of thought. There is a certain uncomfortable easiness in defining the relentless pursuit of peace. It is there in the passions, brimming in warmth, or in the unholy stalking of decadence. The quest, the calm, nirvana, so hard to separate from emptiness. Flee, there is in each day

A disquieting shelter. Keeps you out.

Keeps me out.

Keeps me in.

Sometimes.

JOURNEY 69

Retention of direction,

Quilted skies caress the gathering twilight, inciting innermost insatiability.

Visual dreamscapes draw me, merciless, yearning.

Echoes of each touch reverberate, as the need to breathe is absorbed, then consumed.

The allure of the natural, the carnal, delights and captivates, steals and seduces, occupies and preoccupies till each nerve ending erupts. Tremors drench every pore

As waves of pleasure assuage. Streams of night beams assail the enchantment, imparting nectars of sweet Ambrosia.

Gentle and gliding realms of reality and fantasy dance on charmed eyelids, granting the breath to a love affair of words.

JOURNEY 70

Alone?

Each journey, each moment, hated or feared, made beautiful, or abased, is becoming me.

Impressions sought, cast, or gathered,

Yes, ever present? Restoring sight, seeing light, prevailing in a crucible of emptiness, hey, I see too, my eyes are blue. Destinations defined as each day flows, stealing, into the dark. Relief, a sigh, a revisiting, secret places, innocence refreshed. The passion of the words felt and scribed, veritable healing balms, discovered, allow assurance to the incarcerated soul. Terms of peace, a quip of understatement, still fails to provide a savior. Maybe knowing, bowing to the realization is acquiescence to the need. Sojourns, a day comes, then passes,

As the earth itself. Neither has a concern for what life is supported, nor which survives, or thrives. So, I, search the same heart, and see, each ending is but a beginning.

JOURNEY 71

Feeling the need to run from the demons, I am gripped with unconscionable fear. Lies, lies, of the inner junkie, psychotic foreplay. Falling, broken dreams, strangers, living together, arriving, finally arranging to meet.

How have I not known?

Will I like you? Does this dawning ascend in triumph? Demons dancing in the darkness, will they stir? Facing the contemplation of union, anxious questions greet each caller. Betrayal, so long the victor, threatens to snuff the very breath. Fronting infirmity begs the calling of mercy, a surreal savior. Recompense of sin, inadvertent, reconciliation to an unknown god. Desperation skates onto ice warmed and thinned by nowhere else to turn. To remain, to continue, tragedy's jaws gape open to sanction premeditated ruin.

One final relationship, naked, stripped, exposed. A single choice, to be condemned by the sin, or saved by the infirmity.

JOURNEY 72

How does one such as I pay homage due with accountability? To reckon with justice, to accept tender mercies, Is not easily undertaken, nor is it comfortable. Blind by virtue of a birthing veil, trailing shadows of pre-mortal patterns. Unequivocal dependence dons to a morn of infancy. Not knowing that there is an unknown. Each of us subject to, object of parental Love, byways beyond vision, challenging even the well traveled. Parental motives, never less than abundantly intentioned. Bestow forgiveness without reservation.

The babe, different from conception, same heavenly preparation, this spirit quelled, in favor of a misunderstood genetic confluence. Disquieted disruption, a new rule, outside. Preschool, longings and belongings, emotions, decisions formed and stored, a veritable reservoir of untamed contrition. Saving and waiting, human wills engaging. Heaven and angels guarding, each day shrinking,

This perfect plan, so hard in the unveiling. Lines drawn, etched in to sands drifting, yet uncross able in reconciliation. Youthful brilliance, self-dimming to forge retreats, Pangs of conforming fall to cries of 'touch me'. 'Just me, touch just me', then become easy prey to an unknown ravenous internal predator. Blue eyes, bulwarks of light,

The light of the spirit, the light of the body, 'baby blues', able to shine, able to cloak The growing isolation, without ceremony. Patterns of denial, more easily accepted, Now a trademark of relationships.

From the exterior, friends come to go, siblings fear a crossing, and safe keep a distance. Marriage vows shaken to a core, my own children, so hurt with me, Estrangement finalized in a heart, sequestered by infirmity, To the bidding of farewell to my own 'baby blues', to perhaps, spare what are many for one, so miserable. Inconceivable, the depths desired, even sought, to penetrate and alleviate a life.

And now, only the fear of the fears has the strength to change what may be. To what now is maturing as a lifetime, the wonder of those who have stayed and tried elucidates me, there must be life anew.

To then know, it is not newness, but a refreshing. To that knowing, each in turn, self denying, touched with pure motive, never to malign. Such a thought, at a juncture so wandered, 'With wellness then, may I revisit my generation?' Answers of time and timelessness, motives discerned, Burdens shift, clarity seen as thresholds of truth emerge. The undoing, this undertaking, brings us home, even if home is simply knowing what we never did before.

JOURNEY 73

Agrarian life rings dangle from lines dropped without response. Can you from your place of exoteric expectation curb my conundrum? Pre-absorption, my endless Placards of personality, benchmarks of who we are, Who we want to be seen as, Rule in our casual talk of each other. Pastoral articulations, prayers, unspoken Ascensions Must surpass or at least find credence in a servile heart. Tarnished penetration, or the pretense of such, measured by assignment, or calling falls to fodder. The face of protection, what I allow you to see, to be, to me, is love. Reformation, and the evolution of the front, the face, Chills as it enters, challenges what we know. For there is no knowing, just the allowance to Mend. The love I know adulates the smile, allows the Cure, diminishes even genuine beginnings, euthanizes time, then kindly forgets.

JOURNEY 74

Can a shadow cast a shadow? Doubt, in its most visible version, is the shadow Of Truth, how then can a shadow of a doubt have place? Ringing a sacred chord, an expression beyond every fiber of one's being', and I simply can't conceive of such introspection. Socially mobile, open, yet not available,

Phrases of pleasant compatibility, However, never willing to 'rub shoulders'. What medium conveys truth? Words? Wishes? Written clichés, are they assigned by bureau or committee? Then supplicate for temporary permanence, or slow Death by words.

Old, beaten, destitute utterances, luster lost, shiny as the suit on the old man, like the last snow on an old mountain. To leave what is well and fair alone. To give just to give, knowing motive to be pure, without rancor. To bid latent exoneration and allow such a wish residence.

JOURNEY 75

Fault lines, natural fissures, at one time tested, even cracked, Tectonic plates, heaving masses of earth pressing on The other, Thrust quakes, compress points of weakness on the Fault line. We can pretend to build for it… Can we really prepare, predict, project? An arrogant pomposity presumes such animation. Moods, personal rifts, tried by circumstance, become predictable. Relationships, base human emotions, bodies crowding, Stressing lines in a crucible of forces at the apex. Protected, fortified, delicate personal lines reveal stress fractures, when tried. 'Tis not if, but when, we shall shake our very willingness to withstand, and to rebuild, if not destroyed. Forces that rule our world draw the parallels and provide The blueprints for what then is our interpretation.

A quake, ripping and tearing the natural serenity alone is void of emotion. We judge, we pretend or project and even plan, or we don't, and our equanimity, by design or default, Defines.

JOURNEY 76

The torment of self-infliction, too late to change what is. Acquiescing to the muffled strangeness, foreign darkness engulfs. Searing glimpses flash behind eyelids stitched shut.

Morbid dryness shocks a tongue pressing, unavailing, at lips sewn at the flesh. Surely a tingle felt, toes, fingers, may be detected, must be seen. Parched at every inner pore, the soft scream of death pulses without reception. Deceased, absence of life, this apparent choice to retreat, hastening decrees not to be made, final resting, not finding rest, but to hide 'Neath the demise.

JOURNEY 77

Chasing sunspot shadows, the nebulous profiles

That linger after the flash.

Stop them, blink them back as they flee, hold onto the light as it flows across vision's field. Then there are the times just to squint so strenuously that the flow of tiny darting stars of light fade to dark.

Open slowly, see within that world as it passes into first the pain of gray, then the relief of restoration.

So, why do it?

Why look at a clock?

Why pursue a venture? Why do anything?

Go ahead, catch a sun shape, for a moment, then let it out.

JOURNEY 78

And why not write tonight? The curse of an idle Saturday rests thick, makes us sick.

But, don't focus so much on the dark…

Write of laughter and family portraits. Not of punishing, of where angels fear to tread. But, they watch the descent, maybe weep, maybe just turn a sweeping distance. I look for light, and paranoia creeps, and I become afraid of what I hear in your voice. I need to get out of here, but the calm, and I sleep. It is not you, you want this dream to fulfill. I am so eluded by the dream I am to be, and only seek to ravage, even altered. Night, and its permeating still, hosts the advent of a good argument. The door slams to cajoling jeers, saved, as if stored up and exploded. In the wintry silence, a walk, luminaries guide partygoers, to a Leviticus and booze soaked tribute to the Royal Birth.

The thought occurs, 'Who's right in all this mess?'

The need to disagree softens with each breath, and I notice the dry cold breeze and cracks in my lips. There are others out tonight, each with something to validate.

What have I to prove?

I know it is too cold to solve this in my solitary gait. Re-entering through the portal that earlier confirmed The anger, this time emptiness, sought, unweed, prevails.

JOURNEY 79

Retracing steps that unlock a treasure trove hidden

Over forty years. Each is always there, harshly denied.

Finding a place to release the words to the surface is life.

No one can take you, no one can make you. The places as the events slip, through the common to be lost, if not lettered, scribed as fleeting memoirs. It isn't the events, but the take, not the time, but the memory. In the whole scheme, which moods are truly voluntary? So much effort to take the edges off, what if I like the edges? How can the lack of rage equal the solution of peace?

Hidden shores, coves where the waters of the soul

Capture and hold the thick sludge of waves lapping as the last light of day refusing to release the viscous murk as if viewed from beneath the water in a state that is neither awake nor asleep. It is familiar to retrieve pain, it is likely to force the enigma that each ego fronts. Some view this anathema, run, cloak with religion, blame it on the lady in the tower and deny. From where I sit, the daydream is real.

JOURNEY 80

Common reconciliation sought, values of direction nebulous through the curtains of time.

The journey that unveils the origins of the hidden, the hiding, The masking of the void leads to what? Self-castigating and spurious dispositions smile, and the shallow world of kin accept a victory, a quieting. The cure, then, is the not seeing, remediation, the placebo, is obliquely blind. The quintessence of the initial healing, was to not heal at all.

It was only to draw the surrounding humanity to a perceived analogous affliction.

To feel nothing, to dwell protected without the fringes of societal influence is guarded bliss, but in the nocturne... no masks, no victory, no cure, no remediation... As it were, and as it has forever been. Containment failing as the ramparts erode, human costs escalate beyond the means to pay. Maturity and surrender, hand in hand, seeking salvation,

Expensive and diagnosed voodoo... is it here? Vindication finding rest in induced euphoria, and the gain?

A deep, buried sleep fills the night, a requiem calm comes with the morn. Worth and wonders, new queries to ponder. From here, the sun's heat rises without rage. The lesser light of the night simply soothes. Betimes, a strangers gaze is passed between us, hardly noticed.

And, by this panacea, has forever changed?

JOURNEY 81

Prey to a fantasy, an early morning overture, four a.m. and the alarm's contentious call soothes and coats as warm honey. To feel the coursing of blood heightened and eager, 'tis as liquid energy, giver of life.

Rituals of the tenebrous darkness, the chill of slipping out of the comforter, the blindness, imagined, no lights, just touch, dressing silently, stealing moments alone, almost.

A glance, as you sleep, roll over, and fill my space. A smile, and I continue 'til in readiness, the bedroom, now yours, still you slumber. I know these halls by every footfall, moving, caressing the air, a shiver, counting the stairs, finding the hard wood. A brief departure to turn up the heat, looking forward to the returning. Gazing through the plated glass, the cold reflects back thru a fogged lens. Stepping outside, first breath, wintry.

Driving, musing still, memories flood the landscape of what happened last night, and before.

I trust, yet push limits of uncompromising love.

Do you believe as I do, that today outshines the last? Coming to rest at my destination, the question lingers.

Forgiveness and the falling of a lazy snow enrapture this tranquil voyage. There is no harm in the gentle flakes that light only to melt and be swept away from my view. You, tarry still, I have so much to learn.

JOURNEY 82

From a state of midnight slumber, on the eve of Christmas eve,

Comes to rest, words, keen and sharp, and I ponder,

Too.

But it is easy to roll over, let the thought slip Through

The pillow softness,

And purposefully forget, now as always, for I have lost Faith. The message, the season, the accumulating blessings, How is God and how am I with God?

When will I come back?

Do I know?

Pre-dawn moon rules in this cold world of winter. Sun's streaks, void of any warmth, highlight the peaks To filling the moon shadows on the frigid earth. Even still, this moon stays to witness the morn. Radio waves carry the lyrical ballads of Christmas. Carols and exultations from artists and performers Who indulge in the perverted and disavow such words. Who am I to say anyway? Christmas eve, battling for a safe place,

JOURNEY 83

To know right, by birth, by predicated tradition, then to struggle with inner voices of malcontent, Comes visions of destiny lost. Or at least, forgotten, blurred in the tussle. Transcending a lineage of trusted tutelage, supervised from the perspective of the confines of frames of reference, not with guile, but intents, unstained.

What of the arrival at such an age of question, brimming with conflict, not believing it ever could or should be. But it is, an age welling with youthful hope, and reeling with maturing reality. Deity, hidden in faith, tugs for space, strong and virtuous, yearning to retain the prize, humanity. Carnality and the world vies vigorously at the apex, never to relinquish, ever darkly brilliant in stratagem.

The choice, falls still.

To laugh with derision at either end, is to deny the spectrum, to choose then, illuminates the prism. Maybe today, with new clarity, more right may prevail.

Maybe with age, progress, and within, progression.

JOURNEY 84

Depression, bi-polar indigence, Uncontrolled contrition. Enumerated invocations grace who I have become, Yet the hardness of mid-life failure tug mercilessly. Clinging to impoverished submissions make conversion At the façade impassable. Fatigue, at the core, and acceptance of inevitability looms true. The choice, to bind the windows of my world and it's measurement Or accept the sinkholes of my own humanity.

My own wonderment is if it is possible, or just another shutter of time to hide what may be. Truth, meted in time, and what is, just is, and the repressive world passes to the brilliant, unsuspecting.

Souls silenced, crowding the passages, weeps for the eyes of generation next, gripped with trepidation. Blue mountains, distant, elusive, no, not blue, just Hiding to follow the peaks thru each vale, and rebirth The beautiful. Inscriptions of loveliness, posturing the stoic, challenging to laminating, hopeful to tears, clinging to years.

JOURNEY 85

Stimulus, the sense of being, such a cover, such a foregone regret. The sun's indifferent wintry ray plays with, flirts with each cloud, Each snowy peak, without a visible stir. Incredible sights of visual grandeur pass without notice, Yet to deny the grandiosity, no, just let it pass. I have known to feel for the wonder, I have grasped to believe in the miracles. The things life is lived for, just fade, making life what? Sensation, splendor, just simple moments that chronicle, Slip from what even matters, and I thought it did, once. What do I care? Somebody will see, worship, 'tis not the event that goes meaningless. It is making it really feel, How do I care, when it just passes with forbearance. The tones permeate, betimes, and the velvet touch, Is to soothe and appease the need. Quiet remains as dimensions of mania don't speak back, Just remind me someone else knows all these things. I see the same butterfly, differently each time. Lightly, as a flutter-bye, then as a waste of time, Life so short, beauty so fleeting. It is not enough to give up, to give in, but what is Enough?

JOURNEY 86

Discernment of choice,

Imaginary influences, influenced images, is there a difference? Life changes to open portals of spirit, streaming rays, soul prints rest, uncommon introductions, what is basic and what is wanted? Man at the core, Divinity tugs for latent heartstrings grown apathetic and pathetic, even corrupt. Materiality and the pursuit of the rights of age, relentlessly hold sacred vigils of bidding, blur to ground held, by desperation. Desire, the honest aspiration to seek truth, Can the soul recognize the difference? Strip the carnality of time and what has been, and truly see to change with certainty.

To assess and judge another's heart lies without rights of one looking in. To irrepressibly cast sentence upon another's way, the dilution serves to benefit only the images. Gazing, with hope to atone, self to inner self, spirit to mortality, worthy, if not required for lucidity, serves but to refresh, forgive, and finally, forget.

JOURNEY 87

To speak of love,

I draw frames of openness, of words caressed by tongues of selflessness.

Visions of the utopic, what I should be, cloud my vision on life's highway, overcome me to tears in times when arms and lips are so distant.

To hope of love,

Homage paid to the unsung companion, so hard to say, the sting of selfishness, the refusing to accept right for right, and the intentions of conciliation, fall short to unplanned dictates of habits, molded by the flaws of character.

To know of love,

Simple, yet so difficult moments of speech intended to soothe and calm, find the callous of years, deafness permeates. Expressions dreamed of, find distrust as what is known, becomes expected.

In the unfolding of such love.

To breathe of love,

To leave the reminders of time touched by what cannot be unsaid.

To start a course, removing the fetters of an oppressive hurt.

Eternity awaits the doing, while knowing the ending.

JOURNEY 88

The Pittsburgh Dad, the cyclical mate, the condemning man seeking a stable level. The obedient servant, the gracious Mother, knowing there another son to be. Knowing together only change to be the only constant, recalcitrance bows to reason. A beginning scarred by Dad, working, feigning, convicting. This year of castigating choice, why? Early evidence of wincing unrest. So far away, the Mother takes all these feelings into her heart and believes... Mischief, unmistakably touched by surrounding discord and trailing a soul of an unbridled angel, seeds of doubt and questions of self worth seep into hidden places. Ah, but the Mother, feels his little boy hurts, and knows, everyday, she knows. The moves come, with frequency: New York, Grandma's, Seattle, Salt Lake, Dallas, Boise, Denver, Cheyenne, Brigham City, Oklahoma City, Heber City. Heber City, to watch his Mother bear the insults of a new master soul breaker. Another move, same town, same malevolence, more intent from more small minds, who believe turf has ownership, and different is fearful. Time slips through vivid and visual consciousness,

But not to the young man and his fragile, sometimes

Faltering ego. Each slur, without regard from the ignorance, finds lodging. Let it go, this time. What can we do, anyway? To the evidences, so on display, the Dad wants to catch up, and, now faces the summation of your still tender age. Shortcomings, and the collective result have no motive of malice.

We, who watched, and refused to condemn, now allow, no, we participate in that which we see. But, we know each our own heart, whether admitted or denied, and so many times we know the others, as family should.

The harsh stains, so inflected by the uncaring... Where then to turn, where then to run. So many places and choices, to flee? The world, the seeming happiness of those just off center, entreat and enrapture. The lure of a lifestyle, yet unexplored, unproven, anarchy, can it really work? To so live without law, sort of, except for those that protect me. To address at more still and unpretentious times, to speak to the underlying distresses o youth.

JOURNEY 89

Seasons of dry testimony, hidden torment, release in a flood of tears, words choked in half sentences. Composure relinquished, grace of public speaking lost In but a moment of exposure, beseeching. Worth of a soul, the wholeness of the ninety nine who are not in open need of healing, so healthy, SO well... But, of the one, finding acceptance of the world, Growing apathy to spirit, gains hold of such. Who will be the physician called out to make well Such an one? And when the one is blood of infirm blood, and healing is not within, Is this new majority of one now squelched from view? Is there a net to break the fall, or by now, is there a Fall at all? As the wave surges to the shore, mighty and distinct at the break point, each, in turn, is diluted and finally absorbed by sands Unaffected, unconcerned, unfeigned. To finally distinguish the moment, qualms and questions loom so large still. Each resonating word and pause echo, yet beg clarity... Was this a moment filled with a spirit of hope, or the despair of pain?

JOURNEY 90

Warm muffins overflow the platter otherwise without service. Scents of morning drench each of us upon awakening And we abide in wondering awe at the hands of Love That envelope us. With celestial fetters, streaming ribbons tie us, bind us, keep us. This family, without obligation, without pretense, found simple peace in each other.

Camilla Mae, our only daughter, to share a name with the Grandma she knew, who cradled her granddaughter As her own flesh, and essence. Hushed now to life, the tenderness of this union breathes still. Though seasons pass, ne'er a day of meaning went unnoticed. As a beacon ever present, ever resonant, our children knew, as we knew that the card would come, and she would not forget... A chapter closing, a remarkable passing. For her, a refreshing, a reunion with Grandpa Bob. For us, memories that flood with warmth the hearts of our little family.

May these words ascend as our prayer of thanks, our last embrace. More than a few times as we reminisce, we have wished all could have been as pure as Grandma Mae.

JOURNEY 91

Wishfully daring to create anxious cogitation descends to frivolous and masquerading. Cursory

Time honored and revered traditional holidays garnished with parades and delivered with pretty wreaths... The drive, over the river and thru the woods, to find a corner, undiscovered, don't bother me. Speaking with rhetorical hollowness gathers altogether wanting timbres, to fall unnoticed, gracefully thankful. Babbled notes of song never scribed dribble in the air, without accord. Content and appeased, conscious awareness escapes need. Judgment external, long since forgotten. The scene, transposing what is beheld, by whom, looms incurably elusive, divided by vales impassable, Separated by experience, so vastly different, eternally. Leave the worth of the season alone, for the partakers. Values posed, unaltered and immutable, lend but a silencing ear. Ebbing indifference comforts spent attempts at a median. Fulfillment abandoned, that which begs the poignant Embraces the absence of rage, with an onerous smile.

JOURNEY 92

Does the sunrise more the brilliant on the wealthy? And the sunset, is the repose of evening a reward meant for prosperity? The gnashing of the gauche indigent writhe as dawn Crests to bring another awakening, another waning day. Enigmatic governance sits as a wicked miser, without regard nor reverence to the more prudent masses. 'Do a good job, boy.' 'Endure the paying of dues.' Of a surety, the rewards follow. Cynical trappings crackle and settle in an abyss, maybe self created and absorbed, who's to judge. Youthful resilience melts to melancholic apathy hardly noticing, with eyes wide open. To recreate the intensity of wanting, to clear the vision of despair, To see the future through the vista of the despot, glassy, calculated, invulnerable, invincible. Insufferable truths that mold the malleable reality.

Then to measure the in-conquerable soul, to Defeat the impenetrable odds, Truly, there is no retreat, no quitting. Resolute and relentless, persevering anew, there is warmth both in vindication and breaking through. A heart void of the velvet dagger fails, I wonder, does this assuring smile give me away?

JOURNEY 93

Outside in... trim side out. Trimmed and decked with the season. This year, something new, please work for me. I just want to see Christmas as the blessed do. Music. Passionate, performed, allowed, continually sought.

Done for someone else's cheer, a gift unsolicited. Filling the house with Jesus name finds a way through possibly the hardest of hearts. Décor. To lose cognizant thought, through a gaze, Capturing slivers of intent, through the lights, past the Santa's sleigh, and reveling in resonant peace. Parties. Accepting the pleasure of pure intent. Wanting and accepting acquaintance of friends. Yielding to feeling, understanding imparted unfettered, as treasures without guard. Gifts. Offerings of honest esteem toast the giver, favor the receiver, in timeless savor. A sigh of intrinsic.

JOURNEY 94

The heart of weighty matters intrinsic press flesh to the untouched, yet touchable. Dreams dreamed, emotions only conjured of how it should feel to truly serve self still evade, Yet beg fulfillment. To cast blame on a punitive God denies existence, Takes mortality to such diminutive lows as to deny That reason or the substance of faith hath place. Faith, defining clarity, aspiring hope, unselfish bliss of giving, Takes flight in a soul's inner sanctum, and is lost to a world Unwilling to seek, no, accept tender mercies so hidden. Mortal reckoning lies within the defining, limiting, teasing the arrogant, silencing the spirit. Lies, passive at best, aggravated at worst, know no difference within, they just abide. To blind, to distance, the seeker from the sought. So intangible, to find relief, So fleeting to reconcile warmth internal with even well intentioned ideology.

So rare to rest in moments so filled and allow the world to sail by without being a part. Of such, the blessing, the need to record and to revere, the sacred reflection. It is with the knowing that the tangible doth return, occupying to preoccupying, that reverence a few words, though falling short, satisfy the sacred need to self sanctify thru such faith.

JOURNEY 95

Waiting for the words.

Knowing the feeling of where words come from. Coveting each, aching to sketch the scene.

Thoughts flit to the peaks, some snow covered, towering, yet dormant.

Then to crystal waters, capturing slivers of a sandstone sunset.

Hues of brilliance fade to crescent moonlight, to lose nothing in silent moments of passing. Reflections on a gilded day, recompense of a silver lining, just reminding a tranquil peace of what slips away without notice. Time wasted, time lost, playing to the souls

Enervation, solitaire on a background of a seascape, meant to be nothing, still irretrievable. Searching for the words to pacify, to justify the means of the constant slippage of time. Minutes file by, seconds as soldiers, to move the hands of time.

So many empty, now just past and gone. Horizons and the hopes of the future brighter lend but hollow sympathy, and still, to remain, waiting for the words.

JOURNEY 96

Again, it is Monday, simple, refreshing, attesting to the surviving of the punishments of the weekend.

Warriors in sin, cloak and complain, 'tis enough for them just to be heard. Tuesday, alive and productive, whirring and buzzing with workplace droning.

The din of the common complaint hushes to the need to make up for Monday's lethargy.

To Wednesday, a truce, a pact, to stay the course, to breathe the energy of a midweek zeal, reason with reality, contribute to the effort.

The flicker of Thursday's mischievous smile, planning the plunder of the weeks end. Placidly scheming, motions barely bringing a complete day, but for the thrill of the beginning. Friday's burden...

To bury the evidence of work at all. Clandestine meetings, golf course re-treating's, warm ups to the trappings of leisure and the binge of pleasure.

It is enough on Saturday to recover, shield the sun's forever glow from slits of puffed eyes begging. Attendance optional to chores that somehow get done without feeling the pain. Sunday's guilt, penitent and pompous, nothing really hidden in Machiavellian confessions.

Contrition knows her own, lays claim to sincerity, and dies in the twilight of a new week's setting sun.

JOURNEY 97

Did you ever look through the years and see today? Early years, dirty diapers, bumps and scrapes. Babies coming, fast and so life filling. So consuming, could you see even past the day? The days, as years. The trials, as tears. Where does the fight come from to soothe and then protect? Giving first aid to the moment, then gazing at the Ceiling into sleepless nights. As choices shift, and directions mattered, Did you feel displaced, unimportant? To just watch now, as moments of adolescent wisdom Serve to guide and steer the lives of your begotten. Your words having melted away, leaving only the velour of the emotions delivered.

Deep and implanted, we ne'er doubted what profoundly has granted love, that we too may pass to a new generation. Even the tough days, passing to pained and tempestuous twilight, still there exists the knowing that each day, each moments counsel, came from the ultimate caring, never an impulse for self overruled a decisions delivery. Memories so numerous as to rival the golden sands

That was the rapture of a Newport Beach Sunset, so ominous as the sandstone dawn on a sunburned Lake Powell Holiday weekend. Do you now see the years as we do? The becoming of each soul, now a blessed generation o immeasurable worth. Can you now capture the day? We honor you, the progenitors of our own happiness, We give our gifts as children of promise. We are entrusted to bear your burdens in ways you made us familiar. My simple gift: words, a few gilded words, adorn life's tapestry warmly. As autumn in New England, each color, each brilliant Fallen leaf Adds to the richness of what is yours, then ours, and

Our children's legacy. Thank you, we love you.

Journeys Karl Hicken

www.ingramcontent.com/pod-product-compliance
Lightning Source LLC
Chambersburg PA
CBHW071116120626
46546CB00003B/1363